Paperback ISBN: 978-0-359-76742-7

Cover Design: Placeit.net

Trust Issues

A Journey of Trusting Past Understanding

By: Chandra D. Coleman

Dedication

This book is dedicated to my husband. Babe we made it. Thank you for pushing me when I wanted to give up. Love you most.

Contents

Introduction

trust

Noun

-The firm belief in the reliability, truth, strength or ability in someone or something;

-belief that someone or something is reliable, good, honest, effective.

Trust is such a fragile thing, but yet oh so strong. Alliances are created on its foundation. Families are strong because of it. Marriages thrive when both spouses protect it. Teams reach championships when they put their trust in their teammate's abilities. It can take years or months to build it, but only a moment to shatter it.

Trust can be a crazy thing. Trust can make a five-year-old child allow her father to swing her above his head, spinning in circles, holding only her arms, and be secure in knowing that he won't sling her fifteen feet away. Trust makes thrill-seekers jump thousands of feet from perfectly good airplanes, because they have no doubt the parachute will operate without a problem. Trust in a best friend will cause you to hop in her car every day for lunch break despite her driving that puts you into tachycardia almost every ride.

Trust will make a person walk away from a job paying six figures to walk into the calling God has placed on them, no matter the pay cut, because they know God will provide.

Whether it's between a husband and wife, a parent and child, between friends or with God, trust is a powerful thing. When we have an undying trust, we feel secure. It's amazing how we can sometimes trust without the slightest ounce of doubt, or any inkling that our trust might be shattered.

We've heard the analogy that we can sit in a chair and trust that it will hold us up, without inspecting the chair or legs before we sit down. If the chair *looks* sturdy, we don't think twice, we just sit. The way we trust inanimate objects can be mind boggling at times if we really ponder it. After first hearing this analogy, it made me wonder why don't we trust in people that way or more so why I don't just trust in God that way?

As I examined my life from childhood until now, how I've experienced heartache in my marriage, ministry, and close relationships; I realized that, be it unforeseen circumstances or seemingly unanswered prayers, trust can be easily broken.

We base our trust on the validity or the *sturdiness* of people, relationships, situations and failed expectations. When life-altering or trust-altering circumstances arise, it can have an impact on the way we view others, ourselves and even God.

This makes trust seems like a foreign thing. Our tendency is to shut down and shut people out. Being alone seems like an easier feat than rebuilding.

The pain from broken bones seem to be more bearable than the pain of broken trust. At least with the bone we can have an idea when to expect the healing and restoring of the bone, but with trust, only God knows when we can truly be healed.

Trust has always been a struggle for me, due to certain things I faced as a young child and teenager. It seemed like I was always suspicious about everyone's intentions towards me and that struggle only grew when I became a mother. I didn't even trust my own husband (then boyfriend) with our first daughter. That mind-bending suspicion caused me to lose friends and kept new friends away. I made sure to keep people from getting too close to me, though I so desired to be loved and accepted by my peers. I was like a tugboat in a river current. I was moved by the love of others but pushed back against the currents at the first sign of closeness or the requirement to trust.

You would think that after coming to know the Lord some of these feelings would have subsided. I didn't call it suspicion anymore, just discernment, because I of course have to protect my heart. Some things just take time to conqueror. As I continued to walk with the Lord my heart started to soften, I made friends and my suspicion slightly died down (but never my discernment). I was actually learning to trust for the first time in my life! After years of struggle it seemed like I could finally breathe! Then came one of those unforeseen circumstances. It came like a hurricane and the shattered pieces of my life hit the ground. It was then I had to learn trust all over again. I was back to square one. All the progress, *kaput*. I was learning this trust thing all over again, but this time it was different. I was learning to trust a someone I couldn't see. I was learning to trust an invisible, but very present, God. I had trusted Him before all the turmoil, but this time

He was asking more of me. God wanted me to trust Him past the pain, past the rage, past circumstance, past my own understanding. The journey was not an easy one, but it has been rewarding one. I hope the words of the pages ahead help you on your journey of trusting past your own understanding. Trusting past it all.

"Trust in the Lord with all your heart and lean not to your own understanding...." Proverbs 3:5a

"We base our trust on the validity or the sturdiness of people, relationships, situations and failed expectations."

Chapter 1

The Struggle to Trust?

"The best way to find out if you can trust somebody is to trust them."

-Ernest Hemingway

If I would have heard that quote years ago, I would have laughed and said yeah right! I was like a tiny fort guarded by rabid dogs and angry fathers with shotguns. I did not desire to let anyone in. Honestly enough, I felt like there weren't many who desired to be close in the first place, so I would punish anyone that even looked like they might want to come inside the tiny fort called my life.

What everyone on the outside didn't know was the rabid dogs and angry fathers on the outside of that tiny fort were nothing but fear of rejection, pain and disappointment. As a little girl I wasn't the most popular kid. I didn't have all the name brand shoes and clothes. I was very shy and awkward, not to add, tall and skinty. (...yes, I said skinty.) A child like me was like a walking target. I was kind of like that ugly duckling story, not so cute growing up, but eventually I turned into a beautiful swan.

But, before that beautiful transformation, I was reminded that I wasn't a swan yet. Kids were mean when I was younger even without social media and cyber bullies. From being called skinny, ugly, flat chested, four-eyes, and even being called Prince (because I had the great idea to cut my hair in middle school), I concluded that everyone was out to get me.

I recall one time in particular when I was in elementary school, I thought I had made a new friend. I was so excited. I finally felt like I was accepted by someone at school. I invited her over for a sleepover and it was so much fun. At least I thought so. When we get back to school the next week, I learned that the girl had went around and told everybody that my house was ugly and that I lived in a shack. Looking back those remarks seem so petty now. But to a little girl who just wanted to be accepted, it was heart-breaking. Needless to say, these things taught me to build walls at a very young age. By the time I was in high school, I was a master mason, building walls one experience at a time.

My high school days were not as nearly dramatic as elementary and middle school, but they were vital in my breakdown of trust towards people. High school was high school. There weren't any really surprising things that transpired. There were fights, rivals, jealousies, pettiness, friendships, sex, pregnancy, high school sweethearts, break-ups, and football.

By this time, I had made some good friends. My social skills had somewhat improved, and I had mastered the appearance of letting someone inside my tiny fort. All the while I was just waiting for them to mess it up. I had my first real boyfriend in freshman year, it lasted all of one year or so? I never trusted him, and it ended. I moved on to other relationships, still looking for something or someone to validate me, but that was hard because I never trusted a thing they said.

Then came my senior year. A tall, thin, young man stealing ice creams after school caught my attention. Yes, I know what you're saying, "But Chandra he was stealing ice cream!" Well if that's not enough to make you giggle... he was also freshman. Granted, he was very handsome… and smooth. The age difference was a red light for me, but he was persistent. So, despite my hesitations, we started a friendship that quickly turned into a high school sweetheart love story. The more time we spent together, the more I fell in love with him. He became my very best friend. This boy got into places of my heart that no one ever had, and the crazy thing was, I felt like he genuinely wanted to be there! It baffled me that I let it get this far. I let my guard down and I was ok with it. I didn't feel like I needed to protect myself anymore, I felt completely secure. I was swooning and I loved it.

As time progressed, we became closer. We had our first child two years after dating (no we weren't married. I ain't claiming to be perfect, just forgiven). Eighteen months after the birth of our first daughter, Yunni, we were married and had our second daughter, Iriana, within the same year of our "I Dos". Years passed by and two more babies followed, our son, Jay and our little bug, Laynah.

We were a tight knit family, but like most young families starting out, we had issues. Though we were not fully equipped with the tools to face all of the challenges that life threw at us, we had trust.

Whether it was losing the car, having little or no groceries, living in rat and roach infested apartments with two toddlers, losing the house, and losing the car again, we stayed solid because we trusted each other. It was in these moments that I learned to lean on my husband and my own abilities. I said I trusted God, but the reality was I trusted myself and my husband more. I trusted that I could go to my daddy and ask for money for groceries. I trusted that I could count on income tax time to come around faithfully to get a new car. I trusted that we could get caught up on bills when my husband got his quarterly bonus from his job. I mean trusted in everything that I could see, but I was to find out that wasn't trust at all.

I am wired to be a very detailed, analytical person. I have to know the whys and hows and the whos and whats and especially, the whens. I *had* to know all the details. This posed a dilemma when I chose to truly walk with the Lord. I experienced seasons of favor, and seasons of testing, but in the back of my mind, I knew there was still an issue. I had seen God do great things. I had people give me that Holy Ghost handshake right when we needed money. I saw people healed. I saw people delivered. I had experienced the forgiveness of God for myself, but I always felt like I was missing out on some of God's greatest treasures. I discovered that those treasures were found in trusting Him.

God's grace allowed me to walk for a season with this semi-trust, but now He was asking for more. He wanted my whole heart. Proverbs 3:5 says, "Trust in the Lord with all your heart and lean not to your own understanding." One day as I sat at my cubicle, He spoke to me clearly, "Chandra, I don't want half-hearted trust." Whole- hearted trust is reckless. It has no boundaries or red flags. It is rooted in knowing the one who you are to trust. And you never really know how to have that reckless, fearless trust until you are in the wilderness with the only one that can be trusted.

Chapter 2

Shattered Trust

The journey to true trust can be a weary one, especially when you feel that you are walking alone because the one you truly trusted had shattered it all.

My husband was my very best friend. He was one person that I never really worried about hurting me. Now there were times that my own insecurities kicked in, but I was never concerned. We had been together since high school. In 2012, after the birth of our last child we both gave our lives to the Lord. It was a huge change for the both of us and we knew it. We worshipped together, served together, prayed together, and were each other's biggest cheerleaders. If I had to dance or speak at an event, he was there. If he had to rap, I was the one on the front row. We simply loved to lift each other up. But there came a time when the busyness of life consumed us. We stopped praying as much together and my husband eventually stopped praying altogether. He began to go through the motions of Christianity, he still loved the Lord, but He had grown complacent. I heard a man of God say, "If the devil can't make you quit, he will make you busy." And that is exactly what the enemy did.

My husband had stepped out in faith, by the leading of the Holy Spirit of course, and started his own business. God was prospering the business quickly. Jeremiah stayed busy even in the so-called slow seasons and I had no complaints. The bills were being paid and we were finally at a point of stability, or so I thought. In addition to the starting his own business, my husband also did a cleaning job on the side. On occasions he would have a young lady come help him. The two became very close. It was a recipe for disaster from the beginning. It was the beginning of the attack. We were about to learn the lesson to always be alert of three things; busyness, boundaries and the attack after the blessing.

There is such a misunderstanding about the enemy when he comes to attack. Some have the mindset that the kingdom of darkness is chaotic and disorderly and flailing his arms around like a school girl at a playground fight. This is far from the truth. Satan is strategic in every attack. He sets up traps, days, months, and even years from the day of his actual assault. He knows weaknesses and strengths, the enemy studies our habits and attitudes. That's why in scripture it says that he is roaming around as a roaring lion seeking whom he may devour. That's why we must stay sober and vigilant.

See, a lion studies his prey before he attacks. He lays in wait for the perfect time to rip his prey to shreds and that's what he did to my husband. In all the busyness, complacency, hidden brokenness, and lack of boundaries, my husband committed adultery.

I was devastated. This was out of his character. I felt like I was married to a stranger. My trust was shattered. Years of building trust and finally trusting someone to love me, felt like an endless web of lies. This was the love of my life, the father of my children. He was the only one I had ever trusted whole heartedly, but maybe that was the problem.

The forty-eight hours following the unraveling of my whole world were a whirlwind of emotions. I began to say to myself, "I don't want to be here with him, he doesn't deserve me. I hate him!" Lyrics of the song "I'll Bust the Windows Out Your Car" would pop into my head as I tried to gather my thoughts (it even happened once while I was praying). I was angry, hurt, confused, and scared. That may seem a little extreme, but it was how I felt. The one person that I knew would never fail me, had failed me. He failed me, and I knew that he felt every bit of it. He was just as broken as I was. Naturally, my first thought was that he's just upset he got caught and it's all an act, but the more I watched his countenance change I knew he was wounded. And even though he had hurt me to my very core, it pained me to see him hurting. I could tell that he felt worthless and didn't have the desire to live, but I didn't know how strong those feelings were until one night, while the wounds were still fresh, I called for him and he didn't answer.

Moments before I had told him that I couldn't stay with him and that I wasn't sure what to do. So, I figured he had walked outside, maybe to cry or pray or scream. But when I found him, he wasn't doing any of those things. He was standing beside his truck, hunched over, and he looked up at me and the man I saw was not my husband. Those kind eyes were gone, and they were filled with a darkness I can't explained. He was different, and I knew something wasn't right, but my anger caused me to look past it, and I proceeded to tell him "I'm leaving and I'm taking the kids." With that look still in his eyes, he stared at me and nodded. He never said a word. Then I looked down in his hands and there was a loaded pistol with his finger on the trigger. I reached for the gun and he pulled back and began to weep. (I later learned that he had put the gun to his head, but I walked outside. Thank God for His timing). In that moment I knew that this was more than an affair, this was a demonic attack on my husband, our marriage, our kids, and our legacy, but what was I supposed to do? All I had left was a marriage that was in pieces and four children that I may have to explain divorce to.

I would usually run to my husband for comfort when anyone upset me, but what was I to do when the one who loved me the most caused the most pain, and is broken, himself. Who else could I look to?

Insanely enough, my world had shattered the day before church. We attended church faithfully, but going this day was a bit much. I had no energy, no sleep, and no desire to worship, pray, or even say "amen". Reluctantly, I dragged myself to church that morning in a teary-eyed fog. I cried the entire service, during praise, during worship, during tithes and offering; I was a broken angry mess. I can't tell you what the pastor preached on or what songs were even sung, but what I can remember clearly is the altar call. Truth is, I didn't care what he preached on, I just knew I had to get to the altar. So, at the first green light, I was there! I planned on going alone, but my husband grabbed my hand and led the way. Our pastor was going around and praying for people, but he walked past us, and motioned for some stranger. I had never seen him before, but the moment he began to pray I felt like he knew us. There was a love and sincerity as he prayed. Then he said six words that probably changed our entire situation, "it's not dead, it's still breathing!" In a moment when I felt like our marriage and family was over, God sent word that it was still breathing. It was hope for me! It was not complete healing, but it was hope. Those words gave me something to hold on to, but I still felt like I needed a second opinion because the pain I felt was just too much to bear.

Days after that time at the altar, I stood between the cars in our driveway with tears rolling down my face and asked a question, "God what do you want me to do?" I knew the word we had received days prior, but my hope was dwindling away with each tear I cried. Being hurt was not part of my plans for marriage, so guidance from the Lord was something I needed. Then God answered me with one word, "stay". There was no explanation, no prophetic word for our future together, just "stay". I took a deep breath and gave God my yes. Now this yes was not a resounding, *skip-to-my-lou yes*. It was simply an obedient *yes* that contained a whole lot of pain and even more anger.

I had moments when I blamed God. I couldn't understand why He couldn't make Jeremiah not do what he did. He could have made his car break down or something! At the very least a little conviction would have been nice. But God will always give us choices and coming to terms with the choices my husband made was hard. I had to constantly make a conscience decision to love because the "feeling" just was not there.

To be honest, even as I write this book the words *adultery* and *affair* still sting when I hear them. But that is part of the journey where I continue to trust Him with my pain and allow Him to use my scars for the healing of others. Learning to be a yielded, broken vessel, to be used to bring Him glory takes constant prayer. Even outside of the pain of the affair, waking up daily and accepting that God wanted to use this part of my life was terrifying. I am a very private person. I have very few friends and I tend to be withdrawn in crowds, if I am not intentional on being social. So, you understand that confirmation after confirmation of "God wants to use this" was not what I wanted to hear. I just wanted it to all go away. I wanted to wake up one morning and find that it was all a nightmare and that my life was still perfect. This was an embarrassment to me and I wanted to keep my mess hidden. For a long time, I tried to pray the memories away. I just wanted everything to like it was. In my futile mind, I saw no way that God could use this. I didn't want God to use it. Then I remembered that this life is not my own. I am in covenant with the Lord, and there has been an exchange. I can't say no to God. So, with a humbled, broken heart I told God *yes.* I wanted to hide all my mess, but it's the messy places that no one wants to talk about, that brings about freedom, deliverance, healing and restoration. That's when I understood that God is truly not about waste.

Psalms 56:8 says, "You keep track of all my sorrows. You have collected all my tears in your bottle. You have recorded each one in your book." The amazing Father we have is intentional about His children. He even keeps our tears! How amazing is that? He will never waste pain, experiences, trials, tears, even death, just ask Lazarus. Even the messy situations in our lives God can use, that is if we are willing to surrender those things to Him. All of our mess, pain and heartbreak can bring Him glory. That's what He desires.

God desires to get glory out of your life. Not only will your story bring glory to God, but it will bring freedom to others if you allow God to use it. The willingness to share your story is like throwing out a life preserver to someone who is drowning. Just think if you were able to look into the spiritual realm and see the people God called you to. If you could see those drowning in their pain and confusion, wouldn't you want to throw out your testimony to show them there is a way to survive? If you were able to look into the spirit realm and see all the people bound by darkness, guilt and shame, and you had the keys, wouldn't you supply them with the keys they need to be free? This is what your story does. Revelation 12:11 says, "And they overcame him by the blood of the Lamb, and by the word of their testimony." Our testimony is not just for our victory and triumph, but also for the victory and triumph of those who hear it.

The willingness to share your story is like throwing out a life preserver to someone who is drowning.

Chapter 3

Trust the Process

If you hate process raise your hand! (insert raised hands emoji) Well let me change that, I don't hate it anymore, but I do have to remind myself to embrace it. Process was one of the hardest things for me in my Christian walk the first few years. I was filled with the Spirit, prophesied over, and was ready to take on the world! What I wasn't prepared for was to be pruned over and over again. I wasn't ready for God to reveal the darkness of my heart and the broken places in my life. I wanted Him to use me to shake nations within a few short weeks of accepting

Him as my Lord and Savior. I was so immature. I didn't understand the growth that needed to take place. If God had positioned me in all the places, with all the people, on all the platforms I was praying for and was promised at that time, it would have ruined me. I was still a baby. I was a full-grown cry baby. I got offended over every little thing and needed people to validate me so badly. I craved for my leaders and peers to telling me how proud they were of me. I wanted them to tell me what they thought I was called to. I longed to be soothed by the extra special statement, "you are so powerful and anointed!" It was a miserable, unstable emotional, whirlwind. The ups-and-downs of waiting on man's word kept me unstable and unhappy. I would do my work unto the Lord, or so I thought, and then turn to my neighbor for a pat on the back.

I came up with this marvelous epiphany; my works will speed up God's process of the promise. The more I served, the more I felt like I was entitled to speedy elevation. Now, don't get me wrong, I loved to serve at my church (I still do), but at the time I would often find myself doing it for applause and advancement rather than heavenly rewards. God had to take me through a process of refining and pruning to remove all the selfish ambition, the people pleasing, the impatience, the dead works, the fear of rejection, the fear of man and the surface living. The process became painful at times because it was cutting away the fleshly desires I had for a long time. I learned I had to be patient and wait for the promises of God. I had to develop tough skin and realize that everybody won't like me. I learned that offense is the rigid stone that smooths out the rigid places of our hearts. I didn't need man to validate me anymore, because my validation came from my identity in Christ. Still there were more processes that I had to and will have to endure in life, but the process of forgiveness, healing, and restoration in my marriage was a process that I truly wanted to speed up.

After the smoke cleared and the dust settled, it was time to put in the hard work in the privacy of our own home. It was fine to put on a smile and hide the pain in public, but at home the questions and emotions were always in play. While I had every right to be angry, hurt, and everything in between, my desire was not to stay there. It was time for healing, praying, fasting, renewing, restoring, fighting, and loving. While I thought that those things would just come naturally, because this was the man I loved, it took a grace and power I did not have. I had to ask God to give me strength every day.

Days seemed to last forever. So did the nights. I felt like I was moving in slow motion all day. It was like an out-of-body experience. I was alive and not living. I wore the perfect mask. This is where God's grace came and flooded my life. I remember sitting at my desk weeping and telling God I couldn't do this much longer. It felt like the life was being drained out of me and it seemed like I was so far away from God. If I'm being honest, this was by choice.

It was in that moment of desperation God led me to a place in His word. I flipped to Hosea 6:2, "In just a short time he will restore us, so that we may live in his presence". It was like God was saying, "If you let Me, I can do this quickly and people will see the miracle of my restoration power. They will see that I can do things in record time, and that my time is not like man's time." I carried this word with me daily. When days seemed longer, because of the pain, I held on to His word. I had to trust the process of God's timing. But trusting the process of His time wasn't the only process.

When tragedy hits, I believe that God takes these opportunities to heal other hidden areas of our life. These times of turmoil are used to shape our hearts. Our very selves are being formed and pruned through the processes of tragedy. It's hard to comprehend that our failures, faults and catastrophes are being used to mold us in the hands of the Great Potter, but that's exactly what happens.

Being shaped and molded from the inside out is not a comfortable process.

The healing process in our marriage also brought about healing within me. All the things that I labeled as "me just being me" had to be dealt with. The anger issues, attitudes, insecurities, and the lack of trust; God was dealing with it all. He was reforming and reshaping my heart. God was changing the way I talked, the way I thought, the way I trusted and the way I loved. I was being made new in Christ... again. Each day God would reveal things to me about myself that couldn't go with me into this new season of life, and my new season of marriage. I felt like I was being stripped of everything Chandra. All of the mindsets that didn't line up with my destiny had to be cast down. The things that seemed just a normal part of my personality were being revealed as blockages in the spirit. I was emptying myself to be filled by Him.

I felt like God needed to deal with all the internal things in my life. While this process was not an easy one, it was so necessary. It's said that for the finger you point, there are three pointing back at you. This was my truth. I wanted God to deal with my husband and his failures. He needed to feel every ounce of pain and remorse, so he could understand the magnitude of his mistakes, but he wasn't the only one. I had to take responsibility for the things I brought into my marriage. I had to repent for things I spoke over my marriage. God not only humbled my husband, He also humbled me. It blew my mind that God was using this mess to bring about the changes I prayed for in marriage and my husband, but not without fixing my heart first. When the prophet Samuel went to anoint the next king God told him, "Do not consider his appearance or his height, for I have rejected him. The Lord does not look at the things people look at. People look at the outward appearance, but the Lord looks at the heart." (1 Samuel 16:7 NIV). Looking like I had it all together wasn't enough for God. He wanted my heart. I couldn't understand why He wanted to bring these things up now. "I thought we were good, God. I don't even see the issues of my past or what that has to do with what's going on right now." Then He spoke, "How can you, still being broken, steward the new gifts, the new husband, the new marriage, and the new love with all of your cracks?" It's just like the new wine skin. You can't put new wine in an old wine skin, and God couldn't put this new love into my old tainted heart.

God has a way of using all of our junk! He was using this pain to walk me through a process of wholeness. This was a wholeness I never knew before, because I thought I was already whole. Broken places, venomous roots, and generational curses, this is what God was dealing with, and I had to trust His process. I had to trust that the pruning away of things long past was for my good. Confronting your faults and shortcomings is not easy when you feel like you are the one who has been wronged.

Some of you may be asking, well Chandra you say trust the process, but how? How do you trust the process? What do you do when the process is still going on for days, months, or maybe even years after you thought it would be well over? The answer my dear is one word…SURRENDER.

At times, we can be so frightened by the unknown and the things that we can't control. So, what should we do? We surrender it all to the one who controls everything. The One that can control the wind and the waves. The One that spoke, and things seen and unseen were, and still are. The One who loved us so much that He sent Himself wrapped in flesh to die for our sins. Deciding to let God be God and trust our very lives to the hands of the One who created us in the first place, is how we trust the process. While surrender may just sound like a dramatic one-time event, it's not and I didn't understand it until God gave me a vision.

I was listening to a sermon about the cross. It was amazing, but for one moment God took me off into a place of revelation. In my vision I saw myself sitting in a living room. It was a familiar place; a place of pain and stolen innocence. As I continued to look, I saw myself now, 33-year-old Chandra. I took the hand of the younger me and led her to the cross. I began to explain to her the cost Christ paid for her. The pain she carried, Christ carried for her to be victorious, and no longer a victim. Then the vision takes me to the park the day I found out about my husband's infidelity and once again, I grabbed my own hand and went to the cross. At first, I wasn't sure what the vision meant, but God later revealed it to me.

See, the thing about being totally surrendered may require trip after trip to the feet of Jesus. It may take seeing His body stretched high and wide to understand that He bore it all so I can take off my cloak of shame and the identity of victim and put on a garment of praise and victory.

So, you must fully surrender, even if it takes several trips to His feet. Keep going until what you need to surrender is all left at the foot of the cross.

"He was using this pain

to walk me through a

process of wholeness."

Chapter 4

Trusting in the Loneliness

I would like to call myself an ambivert. I can be in a crowd of people and have a good time and at the same time be ready to go home get in my pajamas and read or watch a good movie (I'm personally a fan of Marvel Movies). Not only am I an ambivert, I also have somewhat of a hard-headed stubbornness when it comes to asking for help or advice. I'd much rather struggle through with *my* solution, and if should come crashing down then ask for help. Sometimes I even succeed, by God's grace of course.

As I have gotten older, that hard-headedness has become a little harder, and often causes me to push people away altogether. When I push people away on my own terms, I am totally fine with that. When God removes people from my life, I get over that a little quicker these days. when God places me in a season of loneliness and I know when it's Him, I feel it in my bones, and I try to prepare myself the best I can. This what I began to feel for a short time during the restoration of my marriage.

I have some of the most amazing friends. They all have their own personalities that make me love all of them differently. When I found out about the affair, I was so embarrassed. I didn't tell them at first, for fear of what they might think, and for a couple of them, fear of what they might do to my husband. One of them did find out the day that it all came out though. Our husbands are very close, and Jeremiah felt like her husband was the only one he could turn to. So, we spilled everything to them. Not once did she pass judgement. She was there for me.

She held me as I cried. When I told her that I wasn't sure how I was going to move past this, she said something that I will never forget, she said, "Chandra you are going to do it with grace." I didn't see it then, but looking back now, I see that God had given me a supernatural grace to persevere and endure.

Days later, I told another friend, only because God told her something was wrong, and she was always there for me. They all were. Their prayers were felt, but when the loneliness hit, there was nothing I, nor any of my friends could say or do. This was a loneliness that was ordained.

I can recall times talking to my friend, when she would give me advice or correction, and I would feel like she just didn't understand. She didn't know the pain I felt, so how could she tell me what I should or shouldn't do? I wasn't angry with her or the advice she gave, but it just wasn't enough for me. I know that may seem harsh and ungrateful, but it's honest. This made me frustrated because I am usually good about receiving from my close friends and those that I ALLOW to speak into my life, but this was weird. At times I wanted to complain, cry, or just vent to them, but God wouldn't allow it. I felt my lips had been sealed by the angel of the Lord like the prophet Zechariah. Every time I would try to talk about the state of my marriage. Lord would convict me and tell me to be quiet. I wasn't sure why the Lord was doing this, but I knew it was Him. The more I sat in the loneliness, the more I came to realize that the God of all the universe was asking to be my friend. He was asking for me to talk to Him, to confide in and lean on *Him alone*. He wanted me all to Himself. Oh, what love that is from a great Father.

You may ask, "Why would a loving God leave you or make you to feel lonely? His word says that He will never leave you nor forsake you so why would He make you feel all by yourself?" Well, for one I think there is a difference between *alone* and *lonely.* Also, I think God ordains seasons of divine loneliness. Some call them *wilderness experiences*. I like to call them *drawing seasons.* It is in these seasons that no one else will understand you. You feel isolated. Even in a room full of people, you will feel like you don't belong. Even among your best friends you will become frustrated because they can't comprehend your struggle. This is because He is drawing you. He is beckoning you to *be* with Him, not just exist around Him. Drawing seasons are the times when God is revealing things to you about you. Not only is He revealing things about you, He is also revealing the many dynamics of His character to you. You may know Him as Provider, but do you know Him as Healer? You may know Him as a Protector, but do you know Him as a Restorer? He wants you to know HIM! God, the Lover of our soul is calling us deeper and certain things, certain people are just background noise. So, He isolates you to only hear and see Him. We must be careful in these seasons not to allow the enemy to feed us imitation bread. What I mean by this is, when you are in this drawing season, be like Jesus in the wilderness. When Satan came to tempt Him with the misconstrued word, Jesus responded with the true word. So, when the enemy comes in our drawing season to say, "Oh look at you, you are so lonely, and nobody cares about you." We can respond, "I may feel lonely right now, but I am never alone. For He told me that He would never leave me nor forsake me." Don't receive the bread the enemy tries to feed you, not when you have been given the bread of life!

"He is beckoning you to

be with Him, not just

exist around Him."

Chapter 5

Hands Off!!!

Don't touch that! You are going to hurt yourself!

How many parents or adults that spend time around children, can say that these phrases are part of your daily vocabulary? Children have such curious little minds and sometimes those curious little minds cause them harm. I can recall when my second oldest was mesmerized by the wax of a burning candle. She sat and stared at the hot wax and its liquid purple texture. I could tell her mind was trying to figure out exactly how this once solid piece became a liquid by just a small flame. Then she looked over to me and asked, "Momma, what does this wax feel like? What will happen if I touch it?" Now for those who know my Riri, she was then, and still is an experimenter. She likes to see how things work, and what she can make by using different materials. Some of these concoctions she finds from watching YouTube videos, and others she just conjures up in her mind. Her love for science, and vast desire for knowledge has sometimes caused her a little trouble. I instinctively knew that simply answering her question would not be enough, but I did anyway. I firmly told her, "Riri don't touch that! It's hot wax and will burn you. If you touch it, it won't be melted wax anymore, it will be hardened on your hand." She simply nodded her head as if she understood, but I knew it wasn't over. By the time I had gotten up from the couch to walk to the kitchen, I heard, "OWWWW, momma it's hot! Get it off!" She had stuck her finger in the wax! I walked over and peeled the wax from her hand and said, "I told you not to touch it!" And that was the last time she ever touched hot candle wax.

Now while we always tell children, "no, that's hot, don't touch that," how many times do we as adults touch things that God simply said to take our hands off of ? Just like a concerned parent, warning our kids not to touch certain things, God does the same for His children. He's a good Father who cares for His children. He doesn't tell us to remove our hands from certain things because He wants to punish us or keep good things from us, instead it's His divine protection. These are the times when our hands are simply in the way or just too small to accomplish what God desires to accomplish. I thank God for His protection.

I had never thought of myself as a controlling person. My personality is very laid back and chill. However, I learned I was only that way when I was in control. I'm not saying I was rebellious and couldn't follow leadership, but in my own life I was ok, as long as I could control whatever occurred in my life. I like to make plans and see those plans follow through without a hitch. My husband can attest that failed plans were devastating to me. If I had taken the time to make plans, write out plans (because I am also a list maker), and not see those plans follow through as I desired, everybody better duck and run for cover. This posed a huge problem in the restoration process of my marriage and, as I am learning now, in my life in general.

As our restoration process went along, I fell more deeply in love with my husband. I could see the changes in him more and more each day. He was changing right before my eyes. The man I had prayed for was manifesting through all of our mess. He was growing and falling deeper in the love with the Lord. It was an amazing sight to see, but a part of me wanted to push him. Don't get me wrong, encouraging your spouse to be better is a great thing, but corrupt motives behind the encouragement corrupts the good work. My encouragement for my husband wasn't about him bettering himself, it was about me. There were times when I would ask "Did you pray? Have you read the Word today?" I wanted a part in my husband's healing, wholeness, and repentance. At least I thought I did. The truth is I wanted to, or felt like I needed to, be responsible for his walk. I needed him to love the Lord and to love me. Although I wanted my husband to grow and be a great man of God, none of this was coming from simple accountability. It was selfishness and fear. My questions weren't rooted in the desire to see my husband grow in his walk with the Lord, they all stemmed from my fear of pain and disappointment. He had already disappointed me, so now I was simply waiting for the next time he would fail me. It was honestly more like I was setting him up to disappoint me, so that I at least had control over my disappointment. Talk about an emotional mess! Disappointment had become my reality. Sometimes it even felt more like a friend, or like an inheritance. I had received it as my portion in life. At one time or another, I was going to be disappointed by people that I loved. I had accepted it. But if I could have some hand in controlling the disappointment, I could soften the blows, or so I thought.

It sounded like a solid plan at the time, but even now, I see how the enemy used my control issues to keep me bound. My control issues were nothing more than deep-rooted trust issues. I didn't realize the bondage and captivity trust issues can truly cause. I had no idea the bondage that I was truly under. I call it a *silent bondage*. I am not saying that one bondage outranks the other but being bound in your mind and your heart can leave you too crippled to chase after purpose, healing or deliverance. The silent killers, pride, fear, anxiety, insecurity, and worry had become my constant companions. I woke up with them and frequently invited them into even the smallest situations. I thought of them as my friends, but in the spirit realm, they were my masters. I was a slave to my way of thinking, and I was tired of it. I wanted deliverance. I wanted freedom. I wanted the liberty that Christ had died for on the cross. This wasn't going to be an easy feat. This would require me denying who I thought I was, and what I thought I needed, and what I thought I knew and receiving all God wanted for me.

I was truly tired of carrying a burden that wasn't meant for me. I sat at my desk and finally said "Okay God, he's your child. You created him, and you delivered him, so he's in your hands. I trust what you have done in him and I can't do the job you can. I surrender my husband to you." While my mouth said these words easily, my heart was harder to convince. *How was I going to do this?* I was used to doing all *"I"* could to make this marriage work. I said that God was the center and the head of this marriage, but was that true? Did I trust him with my husband? In all honesty if I knew I was working on my husband I could be confident that there was work being done. But was I to trust God to work when I couldn't see Him working? Was this work I was doing, or thought I was doing going to last? The answer was *NO*, a big fat humiliating *NO*.

The work I called myself doing was temporal. I loved the Lord, but I didn't trust him with my husband. My mouth said one thing, but my heart said another. This was a problem. I was saved and filled with the Spirit but couldn't trust God enough with *His own child*. I didn't trust the work like I *said* I did. So, what would my next step be? How was I going to release to God what was His to begin with? A little revelation, that's how.

I began to ask God to reveal to me what I was doing wrong, and how I could relinquish control? How could I make my heart line up with the words I spoke? It wasn't my desire to have a wavering faith in God and His work. I wanted to trust Him. It was a seesaw of faith and emotions. Sometimes I had the faith to believe and the mind to trust, but my heart would fall behind in the rhythm. This is when I began to learn the concept hands off!

One of my favorite shows of all time is the Cosby Show. I still watch every single week! I recall an episode where Elvin was still in his macho-man stages with Sandra. They were newly married, and he still thought certain things were a "man's job". He sat down with Cliff for advice. Cliff's advice was hilarious of course. Cliff simply threw his hands up in a surrendered motion. "If she says she can do it, don't argue just throw your hands up and point at her like, 'ok, you got it'." While this is simply one of my favorite shows, I began to see image and understand what I needed to do in this healing process with my husband. I needed to take my hands off. My hands are nothing compared to the hands of God.

Isaiah 66:2

"For My hand made all these things, Thus all these things came into being," declares the LORD "But to this one I will look, to him who is humble and contrite of spirit, and who trembles at My word."

Psalm 19:1

"The heavens are telling of the glory of God; And their expanse is declaring the work of His hands."

Psalm 138:8

"The LORD will accomplish what concerns me; Your lovingkindness, O LORD, is everlasting; Do not forsake the works of Your hands".

Isaiah 40:12

"Who has measured the waters in the hollow of His hand, And marked off the heavens by the span, And calculated the dust of the earth by the measure, And weighed the mountains in a balance And the hills in a pair of scales?"

1 Chronicles 29:12

"Both riches and honor come from You, and You rule over all, and in Your hand is power and might; and it lies in Your hand to make great and to strengthen everyone."

Isaiah 64:8

"But now, O LORD, You are our Father, We are the clay, and You our potter; And all of us are the work of Your hand."

If His hands are the hands that we read about in the scriptures above and countless more, how can I even think that my hands can accomplish what His can. While as the fleshly people we can be we do try to take on the task of God especially in our own lives and the lives of the ones we love, but our hands are just too small. Sitting at a dinner table talking to my husband I saw what it looked like to attempt to do God's mending. As we sat at the table, I had a vision of an old wooden container, like a barrel with multiple holes. The container was being filled with some type of liquid. As the liquid flowed it begin to seep through the holes. Some of the holes were bigger than others, but they all begin to leak profusely, then there were these pair of hands. They were the small normal size hands for an adult. I begin to see the hands cover the holes, but the more the hands covered the holes the more the liquid seeped through other holes. After a few seconds of the hands frantically moving from leak to leak I saw a large glowing hand. I looked like it was filled with lighting and strong, like the strength of ten men. I knew it was the hand of God. His hand covered every single hole and then God said, "Your hands are just too small." While we are trying to go from hole to hole and wound to wound and heal people and even ourselves, our hands are just too small. This helped me to understand that my husband's true deliverance had nothing to do with what I did and said, it was all in the submission of me taking my hands off and letting God do His best work.

Chapter 6

I Changed My Mind

They say a mind is a terrible thing to waste. While that statement is very true, it neglects the fact that the mind is also the place of the most intense battles. If we are all honest, we have created scenarios, arguments, and failures in our minds long before we even saw the situation arise. Let's be real. How many of us have anticipated an argument and have already figured out our entire rebuttal, with full neck roll, eye roll, hair flip and exit? (Oh…that's just me? Well never mind, I digress.) As I was saying, our mind is a place of intense battle. While the issues of mental health are rising by the day, most battles can be won by simply changing our thought processes and reprogramming our minds. I remember a sermon by the late Myles Munroe, he compared our minds to computers. A computer must sometimes be rebooted, and new software downloaded for it to work properly. When there is an excess amount of "junk" in the computer's brain it has the tendency to slow down, or even completely crash. This is what our minds look like at times. We allow disappointments, pain, bitterness, unforgiveness and deceptions access to our hard drive and we find ourselves with constant virus pop ups such as *offense, hatred, and complacency*. So, what do we need? A mind reboot! A change of mind. We need the mind of Christ!

In the book *Battlefield of the Mind,* Joyce Meyer states, "Positive minds produce positive lives. Negative minds produce negative lives. Positive thoughts are always full of faith and hope. Negative thoughts are always full of fear and doubt." The latter part of this quote was my life. About seventy-five percent of the time, I always had the worst in mind. The boggled-up thoughts up in my mind silently haunted me for a large part of my life. Thinking everything could go wrong caused me to feel like I didn't deserve for anything to go right. If you have had to deal with this intense warfare in your mind, you know what I'm talking about. You know the devastation and fear it brings. You are always too afraid to take a chance or risk because in your mind the worst is the only outcome. Anxiety wakes you up at night, because your mind is constantly going over all the *what-ifs* that end in disaster rather than the *what-ifs* that end in victory. Eventually after all the fights, sleepless nights, fear, anxiety, and missed opportunities, you just get fed up! You finally take stock of all those thoughts; you hold them up to the light and see their flaws. You see the deception of the enemy, and you begin to see the truth. Truth is, those thoughts you had wrapped in fear and disappointment never ended the way you expected. Yeah, you may not get the job you expected. In your mind, you thought it was because you just weren't smart enough, but the *truth* was

God wanted you to start your own million-dollar business. Yeah, you didn't get the house you wanted and prayed for, but the *truth* was God desired more for you. God wanted you to have your dream home built just the way you wanted, from the ground up! Yeah you feel overlooked in ministry and no one is calling on you anymore, but the *truth* is that God is preparing you for the kingdom, and right now, you are just being prepared in the field David. So just worship there.

Our minds become a dump-zone for the lies of the enemy, and sadly we sometimes move some trash out the way only for the enemy to dump more of his lousy lies! Truthfully, it is sometimes easier to believe the lies than to believe the truth, simply because of the way we allow our minds to be wired and shaped by experience and the world around us. I do understand that there are some experiences and challenges we endure way before we can even process the pain correctly. These experiences shape our lives and the way we think. However, there comes a time that we have to take hold of those things and become responsible for our own healing and deliverance, regardless of any other parties that may be involved. 2 Corinthians 10:5 says (NKJV), “casting down arguments and every high thing that exalts itself against the knowledge of God, bringing every thought into captivity to the obedience of Christ”. God’s word is true. It is THE TRUTH and no lie can stand in the light of THE TRUTH.

So how do we cast down the lies? We seek the truth and sometimes the truth hurts, but it always heals.

Walking through the healing process in my marriage caused me to constantly examine each thought. My husband says it like this, “We must put our thoughts on trial.” This was an easy thing for me because I feel like I should have been a CSI agent or some type of detective. The challenge was receiving the truth; the hard evidence. Deciding to think differently would require me to find new thoughts. Those thoughts would have to come from God.

For a while there I was fighting pretty good with my thoughts. I felt like Muhammad Ali in his prime! Right hook! Left hook! BAM! Down goes the enemy! Then came the sneaky deception of the enemy. The bible says there is nothing new under the sun. The devil has no new tricks, just different packages and that's just what he did! He put an old lie in a new package. He used God's word to try and throw me off course! Just like he tried Jesus in the wilderness and did with Adam and Eve in the garden!

I remember having a horrible day. Suddenly, I started to play over the whole scenario in my mind again! *Why me? Why her? How could my husband hurt me the way he did? I was a good wife. Not perfect, but a good wife.* Considering the battle, I knew I needed to fill my mind and spirit with the word of God. So, what do I open the Bible to? Philippians 4:8, "Finally believers, whatever is true" ... and I stopped there. The whispers of the enemy said, "You know it's true that your husband had an affair. You know it's true that he broke your heart. It's true that you still hate the other woman and that he may have even loved her. It's all true!" This is one of Satan's greatest tricks of deception. He was using my own weapon against me! And he almost had me! See, the thing is, he knows the greatest weapon in my arsenal, but he doesn't know the anatomy of it or how to use it the way my commander has taught me. Being a solider in the army of the Lord takes much field training. Hours, days, months, and even years of learning to fight the right way. I had tried every way possible to fight. I fought in my flesh, in my emotions, and even in my words, but this time I knew to fight in the Spirit. I knew the same weapon the enemy was trying to use against me was my sword! I began to quote every scripture I knew by heart. Scriptures that would combat the lies and deception that the enemy was trying to bring about. When I couldn't think of anymore that I had in my memory bank, I pulled out the bible app and searched key words. The more I read, the more I could feel strength and power being imparted. The word of God is a weapon and the more I used it, the more my spine straightened out and the more my head lifted, and suddenly my crown shifted. When I learned to combine the word with prayer it was *game over*! I made the word personal. I began putting my name, the name of my spouse, kids or even my enemies in areas where there was an *I* or *we.* As I started doing this consistently, I would quickly see the manifestation of a lot of my prayers. Not only did I see manifestation of my prayers, it also began to change my mindsets. The more I prayed, spoke, screamed, and even cried out His word, my mind was renewed.

The renewed mind is a mind that has been paid for at the cross. The renewed mind is a surrendered mind. Surrendering my mind to the word of God and to His will helped me to create new thought patterns. I was allowing old thoughts, unfruitful thoughts, and destiny-altering thoughts

The renewed mind is a mind that has been fought for and paid for at the cross. The renewed mind is surrendered mind.

to be washed away by the word of God. As new thought patterns developed in my mind, I started to see new life patterns. The way I simply thought about a thing, situation or person was changing. In some cases where offense, jealousy or anger would normally rise up, I was now showing mercy, grace and even praying for those who hurt me. You might say, "Well Chandra you are a Christian that's what you are supposed to do." I'm just going to be completely honest; that was always a challenge for me. I used to live my life on an emotional rollercoaster and everyone around me was holding the switch, but things were changing. *I* was changing. I wasn't constantly in defense mode. I didn't always think that everyone was out to hurt me. Even if they were, now I wanted to pray for them. The patterns of disfunction, anger, and victim mentality were shattering.

Our thoughts truly do shape our world. Proverbs 23:7 says, "For as he thinketh in his heart, so is he..." (KJV). It's scripture, so you know its truth.

But I'm here to testify, I've seen the fruit of a changed mind and I am living it day by day, grace by grace, and glory to glory. My thoughts started to line up, and life of peace and joy and began to flow all around me. My husband saw changes in me. I remember even coming from an altar call one night at church and my husband saying, "Wow, you look different!" Now that's not to say that I don't have bad days, but when those bad days come, I know how to fight. I simply change my mind.

Chapter 7

He Changed My Heart

I remember always being told as a child that I was soft-hearted. The simplest things would make me cry. If I watched a movie or saw someone else hurting or crying, I would take on their emotion and pain almost immediately. Even when people would cry tears of joy, I would join in. Looking back on that now, I see that it was a heart of purity and love, but as I got older, experiences began to harden my heart. While a good tear-jerker movie could still make me cry like a baby, the other seemed not to affect me like they used to. Seeing people going through pain rarely moved me as in times past. Not to say that I was an emotionless monster, just that my heart was changing and moving away from the pure innocence of caring. It wasn't a sudden thing, it was a slow fade of emotion and compassion, but I thought it was a sign of maturity and not being a big baby anymore. The experience in my marriage placed a spotlight on that very thing. Over just a few short months, through all the healing, restoring in my marriage God begin to work on Chandra; and I mean all of Chandra. He had changed my mind, but now He was coming for my heart.

I didn't know why I didn't see it coming. I was being transformed in every way possible, but there were still things hidden in my heart that God was wanting to heal. At this point, it wasn't so much that God was wanting to necessarily heal my heart, instead He was making my heart like His again. God wanted to take me back to the place of the clay and for me to accept Him as the Potter.

The issues of my heart seemed to become me, and I had accepted them as being ok. The issues in my heart that I had towards myself, my husband, others, and ultimately God were hindering me from a place of true freedom, love, and Sonship. We always hear terms like "girl love yourself", "learn to love yourself" and "best love is self-love", but those things just weren't true in my heart. I knew how to say I love myself, but it was the farthest thing from the truth. My heart and feelings towards myself just weren't the best. I looked in the mirror and saw someone that was less-than, someone that was undeserving and someone that had no purpose. I struggled internally for years. The spirit of rejection had me so bound up that I couldn't even function in some circles. I blamed myself for everything. If we struggled financially, it was my fault; if my kids weren't doing well in school, I was failing as a mother; if someone I loved was angry, it had to be my fault because I just couldn't do anything right. This was my heart towards myself. I was always less, never more; always second, never first. For years I couldn't look in the mirror without picking myself apart physically. (If this was a handwritten book you would be able to see the tears on the pages. God has just done so much! And I'm so grateful!!) I would literally stand in the mirror and critique and tear down His creation, His masterpiece! God needed to deal with it!

Then there were the things I held in my heart towards my husband. Yes, some of those things came along with the infidelity, but God revealed things I held in my heart towards my husband that were created by experiences, fears, and insecurities. Expectations I had for him, myself, and our marriage had been below what God had ordained. Between all this, my heart towards people who had hurt me and, sadly, my heart towards God, He had his work cut out for Him.

As I've already said, I didn't trust anyone. With the lack of trust the comes a heart cloaked in paranoia. *Who's out to get me next? No one has any good intentions towards me.* So, I needed a heart transplant and Ezekiel 36:26 became my song!! "I will give you a new heart and put a new spirit in you; I will remove from you your heart of stone and give you a heart of flesh." (Ezekiel 36:26 NLT). A new heart and a new spirit were what I wanted and needed so desperately, but the removal process was what caused me to stand in the mirror and look past the fake smile and false confidence I tried to portray only *after* I had torn myself down. Even though I had all those ugly, hurtful things in my heart, I turned from the mirror, my husband, or that person and slapped on my Holy masked and would go about my day. But That was just me. Frankly, I feel like God was just sick of the mask and He needed to let me know.

God often speaks to me in visions or things that I see in everyday life, like birds, traffic, billboards, (He even uses Facebook often because I am there way too much!) I can recall lying in my bed one night. This was about the third night of tossing and turning. I wasn't sleepy. In fact, I was fully awake. So, after struggling to fall asleep, I figured God had something to say. I laid in my bed and asked Him. "God what do you have to say to me? It has to be something. You haven't let me sleep for three nights now." That's when it felt like something in the room shifted. God began to reveal all the jealousy and insecurities in my life, and the masks that I put on every day for people around me. All of my silent bondage was now loud! All the things that were keeping me from true deliverance and a close relationship with Him were now at the forefront, and I had to make a choice. I could ignore what was before me or was I could let God be God and set me free. Then He said it... "You will never get deliverance if you don't think you need it. Being delivered takes acknowledgement!" This one simple statement hit me like a ton of bricks. It was just so simple, I wondered why I hadn't gotten this before. Was I that comfortable in my bondage? I had made excuse after excuse for my faulty mindsets, attitudes and insecurities, but the Lord was going for the root. He was coming for my heart. I had learned how to think the right things, but there were also things buried in the dark corners of my heart that arose when no one else was around and a loving father was welcoming me to a life of total freedom and healing.

As I laid in my bed next to my husband, the light of the Lord was shining on places revealing the ugliness. The bitterness that I pushed to the far spaces of my heart, the anger that I had learned to tame for show, and the jealousy that bubbled up, which I masked with excitement for others; ALL of it was now under a magnifying glass. The stony places, the unfruitful places, the weed wrapped places, was about to be tilled up by God and He wasn't going to leave one place unturned. When I heard of the scripture about the stony heart, I visualized a heart that was mean and hurtful, a heart that was unteachable, rebellious, and hateful. That may be true for some people, but in my case, my heart was unfruitful, insecure, and in some cases, delusional. With a heart like that how could the destiny and purpose for my life, and for those who are connected to me be fulfilled? I learned to push all those things back and suppress them long for enough by this point I'd had enough. It was time for FREEDOM.

My heart received all the Lord said that night, but now it was time for action. It was time for deliverance. It was time for acknowledgement. I held on to what the Lord was telling me about deliverance and acknowledgement for about a week. I was afraid and ashamed, but I knew what I needed to do. I needed to confess. This is when I truly began to understand the value of praying, Spirit-filled friends.

I cannot emphasize enough the importance of kingdom friendships. In this life we face many things. Some of those things require agreement and intercession. Get you some friends that will pray you through when you can't even open your mouth. Find friends that will seek God and touch heaven on your behalf. Pray that God sends friends into your life that will truly pray for you and cry out to God on your behalf, not only because they love and care for you, but because they desire to see you win! You need friends that desire to see you free, and long for you to reach your destiny. These are kingdom friends! I thank God for mine!

In addition to prayer, and spirit-filled friends, you must have acknowledgement, Acknowledgement works two ways. It brings humility and it snatches the power from the enemy. When we truly acknowledge, we confess. James 5:16 (AMP) says, "Therefore, confess your sins to one another [your false steps, your offenses], and pray for one another, that you may be healed and restored. The heartfelt and persistent prayer of a righteous man (believer) can accomplish much [when put into action and made effective by God—it is dynamic and can have tremendous power]."

My desire was for healing so, I went to my best friends and told them all that I had been dealing with. Before I could get everything out, my friend Ali asked what had been going on. She had felt something was off with me and had been praying (See, that's the power of a kingdom friendship.) I continued to tell them about the anger, the jealousy, the insecurity, the fear, and I told them about the word God had given me about deliverance. Before I knew it, we were all standing there with tears in our eyes. They began to prophesy over me, both for my present and for my next season. I left them feeling refreshed and expecting for God to do something new, but it didn't end there! Days later, in our Wednesday night service our pastor preached about being thirsty for God. Little did my Pastor know, I came to service thirsty. I was expecting for God to move. I was expecting freedom. As he preached, my heart began to burn. I felt like enough was enough. Yes, I was thirsty for His presence and His power, but more than anything I was thirsty for freedom. When the altars were opened, I immediately stood up and made my way to the altar. I didn't know who was on my left or right. All I knew is that it was my night for freedom.

As I kneeled tears began to roll down my face. Words were few, but I knew that He knew my tears.

The lover of my soul could read each word on every tear that fell from my face. I even tried to muster up some extravagant prayer, but nothing came out, nothing but, "Jesus, please. I'm tired." Every breath that I took seemed like it took more and more out of me, then I felt a hand on my back. It was my best friend Bryanna. She began to pray in the Spirit and the more she prayed, the harder I cried. (You might say it was just emotion, but when someone is truly interceding on your behalf you can throw that "I ain't emotional" mess out the window!) She continued to pray and prophesy over me and then she leaned in a little closer and whispered, "Chan, God says if you want to be free from it you need to run."

Now, let's be clear, your girl don't run unless she's being chased! I do not run for fun, but there was another reason that I didn't want to run. All I could think was," it's there's a lot of folks in here and I am not about to start running around this sanctuary. Nope, ain't happening." This was all going on in my head, who would be looking, what would they say? Then one question from the Lord changed it all, "How bad do you want to be free?" Well, I wanted it bad! I stood up from the altar tears still streaming down my face and I took off!

As I began to run, I felt things falling off my back with every stride. I was literally feeling bondages lose their grip on me. I didn't make it far from the altar but when I stopped running, I began to lift up a triumphant shout! The shout turned into a joyous laugh! I didn't carc who was watching. I had received true freedom from the inside out. My heart was healed! My mind and my heart were aligned with heaven and I could feel it. The freedom from a moment like that cannot be put into words. My heart felt lighter and my head lifted a little higher, but it wasn't out of pride. My head was lifted because there was a crown placed on my head that night. It was a crown that had been mine all along, but that night I found it. I found freedom as an heir of Christ. Roots of pain, hurt, insecurity, anger, and jealousy had been consumed by the fire of God! He restored my soft heart!! I was able to look at people with compassion again. The formerly stony heart was a heart of flesh again; malleable and usable for the glory of God!

I know some of you reading might ask, “Chandra did it really take you running around like a crazy person?” Yes, it did, and let me tell you why. This was a physical manifestation of what I wanted in the Spirit. I wanted to be unhindered, unrestrained, and released like a runner in a race. This moment was like the sound of the starting pistol in a race that I didn’t even realize that I had been losing for years. I was at the starting line waiting for someone to do the running for me, but it wasn’t going to happen that way. This was my race, and this was my chance for victory; the trophy was already waiting for me at the finish line. This was also a chance for me to trust at a new level. Did I really trust God to free me in this way? I sat and questioned it, but He had proven Himself time and time again. So, what did I have to lose? Nothing. The answer is nothing. Instead I had so much more to gain.

Is this not how we are when it comes to deliverance? We want to put in a special order for our deliverance. "Lord, yes I would like to be delivered, but could you get this person to pray for me, don't let me fall out, I don't want to growl or anything like that. I just want to be free from this (fill in the blank). And oh yeah God don't let me have on a dress and don't let my wig fall off and I don't want to be screaming and crying like sister Betty Lou was last Sunday, because it doesn't take all that."

Ok, well it may not sound exactly like that but let's try this. "God, I'm saved, I am a leader, people look up to me. Lord You know I don't like people watching me. So, don't let me run or fall out or dance. Jesus, I need deliverance, but can we just do this when no one is watching. Lord people will see me at the altar and think something is wrong with me."

Hoonnneeeeeyyy listen! Deliverance is not always pretty. It takes us humbling ourselves and making our flesh submit to the Spirit of God! God's desire is for you to be free, but for a moment we need to lay down our wills and our ways and submit to God's strategies to receive a freedom that only God can give. I've learned on my journey to trusting God that He uses the most unlikely ways. I used to wonder why, but now I realize it's all so simple. If He does it in His way, NO MAN can get the glory. Friend, I don't know about you, but I want Him to be glorified in my life, even if it takes me running a lap.

You will never get deliverance

if you don't think you need it.

Being delivered takes

acknowledgement!

Chapter 8

The Trust of an Heir

"And because you are sons, God has sent forth the Spirit of His Son into your hearts, crying out, "Abba, Father!" 7 Therefore you are no longer a slave but a son, and if a son, then an heir of God through Christ." Galatians 4:6,7

"I know who God says I am, what He says I am.
Where He says I'm at, I know who I am

I know who God says I am, what He says I am.
Where He says I'm at, I know who I am

I'm working in power, I'm working miracles

I live a life of favor, for I know who I am

I'm working in power, I'm working miracles

I live a life of favor, for I know who I am."

-Sinach, Nigerian gospel singer

My girl Sinach! She's not really my girl, she has no idea who I am, but this song did it for me! After years of feeling less than, not enough, and confused about who I was, this newfound freedom opened my eyes! I was so used to living far below my rank in the kingdom that I didn't even realize that I didn't just live in the *neighborhood of heaven, I was an heir*. A joint heir with Christ! Being a joint heir means that I have access to certain things as a daughter that prepare me for the things of my future. My Father had good gifts for me stored up, but I didn't know it. There was a father in heaven that had prepared this huge surprise party for me. There weren't any other guests though, just me. There were gifts lined up the walls, all the way to the ceiling! Each one had my name on it. Some boxes said "Chandra", some said,

"My daughter", others said, "my heir", "Ambassador Coleman", "the blessed one", "Chosen", and still others that said "Beloved" and "Friend". These gifts were more than just the tangible blessings such as finances and other things that the eye could see. There were also things stored up that I didn't even have to pray for. He gave them to me just because He loved me. I was His and now I knew it, but it took me taking a spiritual DNA test to know it.

I could center this whole book and my trust issues around the infidelity in my marriage and the healing process. While that is a very powerful testimony, my trust issues went deeper than that. Remember, the trust issues I carried existed long before I even met my husband. While I thought the journey was all about trusting God and people, the truth is, I didn't trust God in EVERY area of my life. I didn't know who I was in Him, so trusting Him fully was a *brand-new* lesson for me to learn.

My friend, trusting God is linked to your identity in Him. When we know who we are in Him, we will trust who He is to us! Spiritual identity crises are running amok among believers today. We know how to pray in the spirit, serve in the church and when to shout Amen, but we don't even understand Who we belong to. When troubles come, we have the tendency to become worried and anxious when God just recently show up on our behalf! We become consumed with popularity and likes because we don't understand we are the Beloved. Feelings get hurt and we can't worship during service because Brother Such-and-Such, Sister So-and-So, and Prophet What-Not didn't come and shake our hand. Is the created's handshake or acknowledgement more important than the presence of the Creator? I mean He's who we are here for anyway, right? I know this sound harsh, it's true. You know how I know? Because that used to be me. My identity was wrapped up in everything else, everyone else and not in my Father. Having my identity rooted in things that would fail me made me feel like a failure. So, you can imagine what happened when the marriage that I almost worshipped, and found my identity in, came crumbling down. This had become more than a fighting for the restoration of my marriage, it became a time of discovery. It's funny how we find out who we really are in turmoil. I literally found that I was cut from a different quarry when I found The Rock at rock bottom.

After the healing of my marriage, my heart, my thoughts, and my mind, I was coming into a Kingdom place. Laying down all the things that people said and that I had even said myself, both good and bad, I was determined to learn what My father had to say about me because I knew that it was the truth. I needed truth, not the opinions of man. I knew opinions and perceptions change, but what God say was the truth and it never changes.

The decision I made took me closing off certain things. One thing that I had to step away from (and you may laugh) was social media. While social media can be a blessing, it can also be the platform for your flaws and other people's success if you allow. It can be a platform for comparison. We live in a very competitive and comparison driven society and social media has a way of pushing the comparison trap. I would watch other people's success so much that I would deem my own engine failure before takeoff! If there wasn't the comparison, there was what I like to call the copycat mindset. This is when you have no idea who God has called you to be, the unique anointing that He has placed on your life, the set group of people that He has called you to, and the specific work that He has set out for you to do. Instead, you start to sound like other people, mimic their anointings, and look at your gifts like they weren't boxed for you! Let's be clear, your copycat anointing *ain't gon get nobody delivered honey*.

We must be smart like David. When it was time to battle Goliath, Saul offered David his very own armor. What an honor it would have been to wear the King's armor! David proceeds to walk in the armor and says, "I cannot walk in these, for I have not tested them." (1 Samuel 17:39). David takes off Saul's armor and, well you know the rest of the story.

David conquered a giant, *with the things God had already given him!* Sometimes we get so caught up in another person's armor/anointing that we don't even realize that's it's our own stones that will conquer the giants!

As I began to see these things in myself, I pulled away and simply asked God, what does Chandra look like to You? Who is she really? He began to show me who I was in Him. The things that I had hated about me so much were the things that He reminded me that He wanted to use. I hated my speaking voice! I was teased for sounding like a man when I was younger, but He told me, "Chandra, your voice carries glory, it's not supposed to be light and airy." When there are things warring against people, I need to have a commander that will call the armies of heaven to attention."

I hated how tall I was! He said Chandra you are a tree planted by the rivers of living water! You will bring forth fruit! The more time I spent with my Father, the more it was like I was standing in front of a mirror. I didn't only see what He saw, I was starting to look more like Him; like royalty. And now that I know Him and look like Him, I trust Him all the more.

Trusting God as His child gives me boldness. You know that one kid that says "Oooo I'mma tell my daddy" and the whole group of kids scatter? Yeah, that's how I feel. I realize that all of heaven is backing me. Storms and issues may come, but as an heir, an ambassador, and a daughter, I know that there is power when I call on the name of Jesus. I know Him as Friend; I know Him as Savior; I know Him as Healer; I know Him as Provider; I know Him as Protector; I know Him as Vindicator; I know Him as Merciful; I know Him as Gracious; I know Him as Peace; I know Him as Strength; I know Him as Comforter; I know Him as Restorer; I know Him as Deliverer; and I know Him as Father! I know sometimes He just smiles down on me and says, "That's my girl!"

Chapter 9

The Entrusted Life

Trusting God at this level, as His child brought me a new peace. I won't be bold and say I worry about nothing and that my life is lollipops and gum drops, but I will say that walking this closely as a daughter of the King allows me to lean on Him a lot more. Having peace, when things are falling apart, is something only God can give. Being under attack, and yet the blows don't completely take your breath away, is the protection of an heir. Weapons form, but they never prosper! All of heaven is fighting for me!

So, I see Jesus differently because I've learned who I am in Him.

This life I live now is not one of uncertainty or confusion. The life I have now, is an entrusted life. Entrust is defined as *to confer a trust on; to commit to another with confidence.* (Dictionary.com) Synonyms for entrust include; *commit, confide, consign, relegate, turn over, hand over, give custody of.* I literally gave God custody! It made perfect sense because I was His child. He was, and is, my Father. My life isn't mine. It belongs to a powerful God in heaven who cares for me and loves me! There is no greater love I can experience on this side of heaven or beyond! The love my husband, the love my children, family and friends give does not measure up to the love I now understand. But I still only partially understand. His love is deeper, wider, higher and vaster than we can know. Still His love is so great! Who would send His son to die a sinner's death, just so I could be with Him in eternity? Who would hang on a cross and take on every sin of the world when He could have called down legions of angels? So, He would be spat on, mocked, beaten, and pierced in His side just to save a people that desire to take His life? What kind of love is that? How can I not trust Jesus with my life when he so freely gave it? They didn't take His life! He simply gave it because He loved!

Walking in a life of trust in the Lord has given me peace that I can't explain. This newfound peace has allowed me to walk through seasons of growth with a confidence that ALL things were working for my good. I recall one morning, after dropping my kids off at school, I was driving home and my mind began to think about the place I was in spiritually. It was a weird place. I had come to know that I was His and an heir, but this season was opening up a new thing. God was showing who He had created me to be and I was growing into her day-by-day. As I turned into our neighborhood tears began to roll down my face. I felt the joy of the Lord fill my car. I was happy that God was shaping me and forming into this powerful woman of God with unique gifts, but that's not why I was crying. I was crying because just a few years ago, this kind of growing and knowing season, would have caused me to be worried, anxious, and bitter. The joy I had was because of the peace that I had. I was content.

Contentment isn't settling or staying. Contentment is growing while in preparation. I was so excited! I called my husband and said, "Babe, for the first time ever, I'm ok with where I am, how God is growing me, and at the rate He is growing me." This was a huge thing for me. Entrusting my past, my present and my future to God was freeing me up of the pain and anxiety of not knowing the next step.

Truth is, God was still using tragedy to create treasure in my life. We were well past the restoration stages in my marriage, and God was still molding and making me into a new woman. Before, every definition of life, marriage, myself, friendships, trust, church, were all given to me by other people, my own self, but not the Lord. Now, there was a redefining of every area of my life taking place. He was still taking broken pieces and making a beautiful masterpiece. I thought He had done so much already, but isn't that just like HIM? He is the God of more! I was reminded of something He shared with me after attending a women's conference with my sister over seven years prior. The theme of the conference was centered around brokenness and being broken before God. I don't remember much from that day, but I do remember feeling my heart burn for the Lord for the first time in my life. In the days following the conference, I would wake up and hear the word *mosaic*. I would be watching TV, cleaning, even in the shower, and hear the word repeatedly. I wasn't sure what it was at first. I really hadn't ever experienced anything like it before. I was hearing the whispers and beckoning of my Father. He was pulling me close to hear revelation. Sitting in my bedroom floor, I opened my ears and heart to what the Lord was trying to speak to me. He began to show me visions mosaic glass art. There were so many colors! They were intricately placed together with beautiful patterns and images. The textures were different in some areas, but none the less, it was beautiful, and I could tell that the artist took his time. Then the Lord spoke to me. "This is your life. There were broken pieces. Pieces that could have been beautiful as a whole, but now that they are broken, I still want to use them. Let Me use the shattered pieces of your life to create something beautiful. This is why I created you! My desire is to get glory out of your life. Allow Me to create something new for you. Don't try to put the pieces back together on your own. Let Me do the work of a great artisan." That day in my bedroom was the first step to my entrusted life. Three weeks later I committed my life fully to the Lord! Years later, I shared this testimony in our Young Adults service through an illustrated sermon. A woman of God came up to me afterwards. She was one of the people who God had sent into our lives during the beginning of our Christian walk to pray for and prophesy over us. She proceeded to tell me the story of when she saw us in service for the first time. As she began to speak, tears rolled down my face. She said, "You know the first time you walked into the church, we sat behind you. God began to show me a kaleidoscope. There were all the little broken pieces inside, the colors were beautiful together. The light began to shine through, and the colors became more vibrant and beautiful and then I knew that God had a great treasure of broken pieces inside you, but the beauty in the brokenness was when you allowed Him to shine through." WOW!

This is what God desires out of your life too! He wants to take all those pieces and make something new! Some pieces He wants to remove, but His ultimate desire is to make something beautiful out of your life. That's what a life committed; a life entrusted is; trusting the Heavenly Designer to mold, make, and create your life into something that brings Him glory. Proverbs 3:5,6 says "Trust in the LORD with all thine heart; and lean not unto thine own understanding. In all thy ways acknowledge him, and he shall direct thy paths." Our level of trust is reflecting in our leaning. Are we totally leaning without the support of our own ideas and ways? Or are we leaning without restraint or hesitation? Are we really doing a for real trust fall with the Lord? Or are we looking back to see exactly where He is and when He's going to catch us? I get it. When life has thrown blow after blow and disappointment after disappointment, you might say, "Chandra it's not that easy." I couldn't agree with you more, but when the burdens are too heavy, we have someone to cast them on and He is well able to handle them.

The latter part of Proverbs 3:5 says, "... and lean not to thine own UNDERSTANDING." This was one of the scriptures that we love to quote and have read countless times, but this one begins to hit differently when I understood what I was trusting in. The scripture says to trust with all thine heart and not your understanding (paraphrased). I trusted only in what I understood. If I didn't understand it, I didn't trust it! Which was such a fallible way of trusting. I don't know everything and neither do you! So how can I trust in my understanding when I'm not all knowing? The omniscient One is who I trust in. He knows the beginning from the end!

The first part of Proverbs 3:5 reads, "Trust in the Lord with all THINE HEART..." How many times have we said we trusted God and really thought that we did until the Holy Ghost helps us take inventory? The trust God desires is FULL hearted trust, all in trust, not halfhearted, "let me help you God" trust. My issue was yes, I trusted Him in the corners of my heart, but you want to know what I trusted more? I trusted my emotions more. I know this chapter is supposed to be about the entrusted life, but we have to addressed this. We can be so driven by our emotions and how we feel that we feed our trust issues. If we are not careful, our emotions can be our god and send us on a winding, uphill road on a dark and stormy night. We become so consumed by them that we don't know which way is up and become unstable in all we do. I learned that those attachments to emotions are sometimes rooted in issues that have not been addressed or where complete healing has not taken place. It is in these instances that we sometimes take responsibility for other people's pain because no one has taken full responsibility for ours. This is manifested in fear of man, fear of rejection, taking blame for other people's anger, feeling that you have always done something wrong, and the need for acceptance. That was all me! My emotions were my god and I trusted them above the one TRUE GOD.. Our emotions are changing daily, they are based on our moods and atmospheres in that moment of time. Submitting these emotions daily or even five times a day to the Holy Spirit will lead us into a place of peace and the entrusted life.

Trusting God with my life does not mean that I have a perfect life. It simply means that I know a Maker in heaven that loves me. He cares about the big details as well as the small. When things seem like they are going south, I can trust that He sees me and is already working things out for my good. I can trust that when I stand in need of anything, He is already there with the solution. In a moment when I can't see my way through and don't understand what my next step is, I can trust that He is giving me wisdom and directing my path. When attacks are on the horizon, I know He will give me discernment and a war plan that will bring victory. And when everything in me wanted to walk away from what I thought was a failed marriage, He showed me that I can trust Him to restore, and the thing about God is the restored piece is always better than the original.

"Contentment isn't settling or

staying.

Contentment is growing while

in preparation."

Chapter 10

What Freedom Looks Like

Deliverance, true deliverance, is a thing only God can give, and you know when you have received it. As I write this book I am simply in awe of God. This is a year's worth of work! At the beginning stages of writing I would get so frustrated with not being done quickly. While some of it was admittedly due to laziness and procrastination, a large part of it was fear, but the bigger picture was God's timing. The always say hindsight is 20/20 and that is the truth Ruth!! Had I have finished this book in one month some things would not be included that God needed, and most importantly, I wouldn't be able to tell you about true deliverance. This book was a deliverance tool for me. I see now that the time at the altar was just a layer of my deliverance. y deliverance from fear!

Plainly put, I was so afraid to write this book. I was afraid that my past would come out, people from my past would come out and tell my story for me and try to taint it with lies. I was terrified that I was being this open and vulnerable. Everyone would know what happen to my marriage, my personal struggles, and what if I fail! Once this thing is out it's out, but then again, once my story is out, it's out. The enemy couldn't use it to cripple me with fear anymore. This was my final lap for deliverance and true trust in the Lord.

This is what my freedom looks like! It looks like me taking back my story from the enemy and giving it to the Lord and letting Him do His work in every person that picks up this book. Freedom looks like trusting God with my life and my journey, not waking up anxious about the next steps or all the bad things that could happen. This newfound freedom is like a breath of air you experience when you reach the drop in a rollercoaster; it takes your breath away, but the subsequent rush of adrenaline brings you to life! This feeling of freedom and trust makes me love differently. It makes me give differently. It makes me worship differently. It makes me praise differently. It makes me forgive differently. It makes me serve differently. It makes me walk differently. It makes me talk differently. It makes me pray and believe differently. When I pray, I approach the throne boldly as an heir and not a slave! I know that I have a loving Father that has set me free! So, I don't beg as a slave, I ask my Father as a child who is confident in the power and strength of her Father and firm in her place as His daughter. What an overwhelming feeling it is to be loved that much by Him.

I love my husband differently because I understand Jesus' love for me. I understand the grace and mercy that has been extended so greatly to me. I understand why, as we walked through our healing process, people would say that there was such as grace on me. It wasn't because I was weak or because I stayed in my marriage, it was because God was imparting His grace in my life. The God of heaven was carrying me like a newborn baby in His grace! Wrapped and clothed in His amazing grace, I was in turn able to show grace in places where I would have before shown bitterness and contempt. It was in this type of grace I learned that I could trust God enough to love my husband without hinderance or fear. What do I mean by that? I trusted God in the fact that He was great enough to change and transform my husband into a man that had repented, and who would fully chase after God. Not only was he going to chase after God, but he would be set free and break generational curses! More than just trusting my husband, I trusted God had done the work in Him.

Looking back on all God has done for me in just a matter of two years is amazing. I see that God has taken my life in the palm of His hand and molded it into something that I could never have imagined for myself. Typically, when you hear someone say my life is greater than I imagined it is because of things accomplished or gained, but what God has given me is so much greater. This freedom gives me power because of the One who freed me. Now I'm bound up in the love of Jesus. Being wrapped up, captivated in His freedom has freed up space in my life. Where bitterness, anger, unforgiveness, offense, and insecurity were taking up residency; love, forgiveness, and wholeness now dwells. This is the type of freedom that allows you to love those who hate you and pray for those who gossip about you. Freedom like this cannot be obtained by simply loving God, but this freedom calls for surrender of the mind will and emotions. This freedom looks like this:

UNHINDERED

UNBOTHERED

UNBURDENED

AND

UNBELIEVEBLY FULL

Chapter 11

The Faithfulness of a Father

In today's society I feel that the role of a father is being played down and almost despised in some cases. With so many single mothers and absent fathers it can often seem hard to see the value in the power of the presence of a father. I am not saying that single mothers are incapable by any means. In fact, two of the women I call my mentors and powerful women of God are single mothers. They have done an amazing job at raising their children in the ways of the Lord and their children still serve

Him to this day. One of their daughters is a worship leader and the other is a youth leader, saxophonist, photographer; well she can just about do everything! So, I am not saying it can't be done without a father, but I am saying the stigma of bad fathers or absent fathers has, in my opinion, muddied our perception of our heavenly father in some cases.

It's often said that some women have daddy issues, but I would dare to say that it is both men and women that carry daddy issues. It's seen in the way we speak to one another, the way we love one another, the way we raise our children, the way we trust each other and even the way we trust God.

Oftentimes when we hear that we can trust God we solely think of trusting Him as our Creator only, but what if we trusted Him as a father? As I began to understand my position as a daughter, I began to see the faithfulness of a good father. My relationship was beyond that of a Sunday-Wednesday visit. It was much more than that. I had a

Father in heaven that had truly never ever failed me, even when I didn't even see it.

Through all my failures and low-points, I realized that He was there every single time. He had always been there as a father, but now I can see Him this way because I know I'm His child. It's like I had found my biological parent, all the while, that had been in the shadows protecting me and watching me and waiting for me to accept that one phone call that would make it all make sense. The times I didn't even know Him and was out doing things that could have left me dead or in jail, He was right there protecting me. In the moments when I felt like I was all alone or had gone to far, He was standing there helping me pick up the pieces of my life and putting me back together. When my marriage had fallen apart, He was there saying, "No, it's okay beloved, I can fix it, trust Me." It's like I can look back on every time that I wept in pain and see He was right there. I can see the time I laid in bed for hours and cried, He was sitting there on the bed next to me with His hand on my shoulder saying, "It's ok I'm here." Or the time that I stood in the kitchen with a knife in my hand ready to end it all, he was right there saying "No please I love you and I have a plan, just let Me heal you." Or the time I stood in my driveway contemplating walking away from my marriage of over ten years and Him simply saying "stay", and now my husband and I stand together more in love than we did the first day we met. More in love and healed from the inside out as a husband and wife and individuals. Such a faithful father He is! He is a fixer of my life. How could I ever doubt that he would He wrap Himself in flesh and be a carpenter?

In each of those moments I had no faith, no hope, no trust, but He remained faithful! His restoring power had nothing to do with where I stood in that moment as far as my faith, it was solely based on His faithfulness. We sing songs of His faithfulness and we even testify of His faithfulness when He shows up when we come up short on a bill or get a refund that we didn't expect at just the right time. While that is His faithfulness at work, I am talking about the faithfulness that shifts your view of Him, it shifts your future because you realize that He is a promise keeper. You can trust God at His word. He is a faithful father!

The faithfulness that He has displayed in my life is not something that is exclusive for Chandra's life. He is no respecter of persons! The faithfulness He has shown me, He wants to show you as well, but will you trust Him? Even when you don't feel like it or can't see the outcome for yourself, will you trust Him? You have nothing at all to lose, but so much to gain. The things He desires to do in your life will sing songs of His faithfulness to all who sees. When we trust Him as a father, we give Him the opportunity to move as a father because we are trusting Him at a level of sonship rather than as a slave or servant.

Let me encourage you, our faithful Father never fails and wants to come and see about you. He desires to make good on all His promises. He can't deny Himself nor can He lie. He has held up His end of the deal in every way possible. He has provided when you needed and withheld when necessary. He has protected you when cried out and sent warring angels to shatter weapons that were being formed that you knew not of. When you felt alone, He was always there and when the crowds seem to close in, He hid you from the trampling! His faithfulness has no end.

If you were to truly take a moment, you would see the threads of faithfulness that have been woven into the fabric of your life creating a tapestry of His goodness. There is not one more faithful or trustworthy. I've seen Him do it and He's still not done. There are yet promises that He has spoken that are to be fulfilled and I wait with great expectation. I know that my faithful Father is going to keep His word and as His child, I trust Him.

"...see the threads of

faithfulness that have been

woven into the fabric of your

life creating a tapestry of His

goodness."

Chapter 12

Reckless Trust

The word *reckless* was not a good thing in my vocabulary. Honestly, the word *reckless* was an equivalent of messy or petty when I was growing up. For example, someone who didn't care about outcomes or causalities would be called reckless. Those were not the people I would choose to hang around. Although, just about any teenager can be reckless at some point. But as this journey of trust became more intense, I felt this one question rise up. "Chandra, what would it look like if you had reckless trust?"

At this point I have learned to trust my husband, myself, some people and God, but what if I took this trust thing to a new level? What if when God said it, that was it and I never revisited His words with a question? What would that life look like? Well I will tell you what it would look like. It would look like this book you are holding in your hand. It would look like a marriage in peace. It looks like not living in fear of being hurt. Although I understand attacks will come, people will be people and the opportunity of offenses will arise, I trust God that He will be all I need in every situation that comes.

When I think of the word *reckless*, I think of careless or wild. That kind of sounds like faith. I don't care what it looks like because I trust God to do His best work in my life. I even feel like sometimes I am on a constant skydive experience with the Lord. In the words of my favorite song by my husband, "I'mma jump off for the leap!" I'm not jumping to conclusions. I am jumping into His goodness, his miracles, peace, and faithfulness!

All the fighting, crying, healing, running and praying taught me this; I can trust God with my life. I can trust Him with the parts that I hate and the parts that I love. Not only can I trust Him, but I can recklessly trust Him because He recklessly loves me.

Being reckless in the way I trust God has caused me to see miracles in my marriage, my kids, my finances, and in our businesses; but more than the miracles, there is peace. When things seem sideways, I can simply say God I trust you, the ball is in your court. I know this seems crazy, but after seeing God move in unprecedented ways when I left it all in His hands help me to realize that for years my reservation of trust was all about my preservation of life. I was trying to preserve something that God had given, but in order to live it fully I had to give it back.

Chapter 13

Prayers for YOU.

I'm sure that some of you that picked up this book have dealt with some of these same issues I have faced. Those things may have caused you to build walls in your life and use your trust issues as a security blanket, but because you trusted me enough to read this book, I believe that you are on the path of freedom. Read the following prayers and make them personal. Read them daily. Read them in faith and I pray that you too will have victory in your life.

Prayer for peace

Father I pray that you give peace where turmoil or torment has tried to reign and rule. Let your peace be my portion and Lord do it in abundance. Let the things in my mind be of great peace and not destruction or distraction. Be the guide of my life Holy Spirit. As I wake each day let your angels clothe me with strength and peace before I even open my eyes. I break the spirit of torment, confusion, distraction, turmoil and depression. Let the spirit of fear and anxiety be broken off right now in the name of Jesus. Hell, remove your hands off my mind and heart for I am God's child in the mighty name of Jesus. Father I pray for a new joy! Let there be a new song in my heart o' Lord. I will sing of your goodness all the days of my life. In Jesus name. Amen

Prayer for Healing

Lord, You are Jehovah Rapha. You are my healer. So, Lord I ask you to heal me right now. You know the pain, you know the sickness, you know the scars, so God I ask you to heal me! I pray that You heal from the inside out Lord. Let diseases dry up! God my inheritance is divine healing and I receive it right now. Jesus did not take one stripe upon His back in vain, but it was all for my healing! Not only physical healing God, but I call forth emotional and spiritual healing. Heal childhood wounds. Heal church hurt. Heal wounds from mental, physical and sexual abuse. Lord make me whole. I will no longer feel emptiness because of what happened, but wholeness in the name of Jesus! I declare that God is restoring purity that was snatched! He is restoring intimacy in my marriage. (Protecting intimacy in my future marriage.) He is restoring! He is making all things new! And I bind the lying devil that tries to impart fear into any victim of sexual abuse!! Fear of hatred, fear of rejection, fear that its going to happen to my kids, fear that I will be like your abuser. I silence the voice of the enemy in the name of Jesus! I pray for supernatural healing in marriages and families! I declare that the spirit of God will give speedy restoration! Love will abide! I bind up the spirit of divorce and division! I call forth healing and unity in the name of Jesus. Amen

Prayer for Restoration

In the Powerful name of Jesus, I pray for restoration. Lord restore the broken places. Lord you are a restorer! Make things new God. Let my mind and heart be restored. Lord my restore home. Restore my family. Restore my marriage. Restore my finances. Let your restoration power spring forth Lord. And Lord don't restore it to its previous state, Lord restore to the double. Let there be more than enough! In places where the enemy tried to steal my family let us be closer than before, where he tried to steal marriages, let us love and be in unity like never before, where he tried to steal finances, Lord I ask you to send the increase with interest. Lord be a restorer in my life, I pray! In Jesus name. Amen.

Prayer for Deliverance

Lord I need your deliverance power.

Lord free me from bondages that have hindered my destiny, peace, and family. Lord give me understanding in the places I need deliverance. Don't let me be so prideful that I think that I am no longer in need of deliverance. Lord free the person in the pulpit, the pew, and the place they think is beyond deliverance. Lord I break the enemy's hold on over my children in the name of Jesus. I break his hands so that he would lose his grip and I crush his ankles so that he cannot run rimshot in my life. Lord I pray for deliverance from hatred, jealousy, lying, perversion, addiction, complacency, deception, fear, anxiety, racism, witchcraft, anger, pornography, lust, and depression. Let the deliverance of the Lord be strong in my life. Lord let me humble and submit myself unto your will for my life. In Jesus name. Amen.

Prayer for Forgiveness

Father teach me true forgiveness. Give me the courage and heart to forgive those who have hurt me. Give me the grace to forgive when there is no apology given. Let me be compassionate in the places I could be spiteful. Give me a true gift of forgiveness. I bind up every offense and Lord I loose forgiveness. I bind up bitterness and I loose joy. I bind up hatred and loose love and compassion. Gracious God I pray that you bless those who have cursed and hurt me. In moments when the act of forgiving seems impossible, Lord let me be reminded of the way You have forgiven me. Lord I thank you for this and it's in the name of Jesus we pray. Amen.

Prayer for Trust

Lord give me a true revelation of what trust looks like. Yes, Lord I desire trust in my marriage and relationship, but Lord teach me to truly trust you. Lord I place my hope in you. You have me in the palm of your hand and have never left me alone. In times when I don't see or hear or feel you, Lord let me understand that I can trust you. As you have said in your word, let me not lean to my own understanding or plans, but let me lean on you, for you are a faithful Father. Then as I trust in you, you will give me discernment in all things and protect me because I trust You to be a good Father. Worry and fear shall not be my portion! When I placed my faith in you, my inheritance changed! I can know be sure that you will keep me, provide for me, protect me, and heal me! For this is our inheritance from a Father we can trust!

Prayer for Marriages

Lord, I lift to you my marriage/future marriage. Lord I ask that you place your love my heart as well as my spouse. I pray that our bond would grow stronger. I pray for protection over our union. Let us be more in love than the day we first met. Let wisdom and understanding be in our hearts towards one another.

Teach us to love each other uniquely as we are two unique beings. Show us how to be selfless in times we could be selfish. Give us the heart of a servant. Not to be beneath one another, but to simply place each other person before ourselves. I pray against attacks of division, confusion, temptation, lust, and any other plot from hell that has been designed to thwart our marital purpose. I pray that we learn to live peaceably with one another. I declare the husband shall lead as the man of God and the priest of the home. He will wash his wife with the word, loving her a Christ loves the church. The woman shall be a true helpmate. She will not feel less than, but she will know her unique call and purpose as the wife. She will be a woman of virtue and honor. I declare wholeness and healing over us both. I bind up every generational curse that may try to come through our bloodline! I DECLARE A HOLY BLOODLINE STARTS WITH US.